flood

Water police patrol in front of the aptly named Swamp Store in Rockhampton.

flood

Stories and images from the ABC of survival, loss and courage during the Queensland floods

ABC
Books

Where possible, photographs relate to the accompanying text; when such photographs were not available, the publisher has used other images to demonstrate the impact of the floods.

 The ABC 'Wave' device is a trademark of the Australian Broadcasting Corporation and is used under licence by HarperCollinsPublishers Australia.

First published in Australia in 2011
by HarperCollinsPublishers Australia Pty Limited
ABN 36 009 913 517
www.harpercollins.com.au

HarperCollinsPublishers
25 Ryde Road, Pymble, Sydney, NSW 2073, Australia
31 View Road, Glenfield, Auckland 0627, New Zealand
A 53, Sector 57, NOIDA, UP, India
77–85 Fulham Palace Road, London W6 8JB, United Kingdom
2 Bloor Street East, 20th floor, Toronto, Ontario M4W 1A8, Canada
10 East 53rd Street, New York NY 10022, USA

National Library of Australia Cataloguing-in-Publication data:

Flood : stories and images from the ABC of survival, loss
and courage during the Queensland
floods / Scott Bevan ... [et al.]

9780733330360 (pbk.)
Floods – Queensland – Pictorial works.
Natural disasters – Queensland.

Other Authors/Contributors: Bevan, Scott, 1964-
Australian Broadcasting Corporation.

363.349309943

Cover photograph by Alice Roberts
Produced by Red Hill Publishing (www.redhillpublishing.com)
Designed by Gayna Murphy
Printed and bound in Australia by Graphic Print Group

5 4 3 2 1 09 10 11 12

Map of flood-affected areas
JANUARY 2011

KEY

Major flooding

Moderate flooding

Minor flooding

High water level

Cartography by MAPgraphics Pty Ltd

MESSAGE FROM THE PREMIER OF QUEENSLAND

AS WE WEEP FOR WHAT WE HAVE LOST AND WE CONFRONT THE CHALLENGE THAT IS BEFORE US, I WANT US TO REMEMBER WHO WE ARE. WE ARE QUEENSLANDERS.

We're the people that they breed tough north of the border. We're the ones they knock down and we get up again.

I said those words on the day the Brisbane River peaked, when emotions were high. I think many of us felt fear and disbelief at the extent of what Mother Nature had thrown at us.

From our capital city Brisbane, to regional centres like Toowoomba, Rockhampton and Bundaberg, to some of our smallest towns like Theodore, Condamine and Grantham, these floodwaters have left a trail of devastation and heartbreak.

We have faced a terrible test and Queenslanders can be proud of their response.

Our emergency services are among the best in the world and our police, our defence forces, our SES volunteers and the army of civilians who cleaned mud

from our homes are heroes. The ABC also played an incredibly important role during the flooding disaster, broadcasting regular updates across the state.

When an event like this happens, you see the best come out in people and we've seen it already: people out there helping their neighbours – a mud army – helping us back to our feet and showing the world what we are made of.

We now face a reconstruction task of post-war proportions. And we face that task with the steely determination it will require to overcome the destruction these floods have left behind. The reconstruction will take many months, maybe even years, but there is something each of us can do to make a difference right now and that is make a donation to the Premier's Disaster Relief Appeal.

The generosity of Australians has been remarkable. I know you have been digging deep, but my message is, we need you to keep digging. If you are moved by what you see in this book I'm asking you to think about giving again. Please think about making any contribution that you can.

Donations can be made on the Queensland Government website: www.qld.gov.au/floods.

Anna Bligh MP
PREMIER OF QUEENSLAND
1 February 2011

Stories and images from the ABC of survival, loss and courage during the Queensland floods

contents

facing the
deluge

IT WON'T FLOOD

by Jo Joyce

ABC Cross Media Reporter/Producer and part of the ABC flood recovery team

I WAS IN SYDNEY FOR CHRISTMAS WHEN I HEARD THAT MY HOMETOWN OF THEODORE WAS 'ALL OVER THE NEWS'. I LAUGHED AND ASSURED PEOPLE IT WAS ALL MEDIA HYPE.

My family are fourth generation graziers with 35 km of the Dawson River running through our property. I spent my childhood in that river; it simply doesn't flood that high. Theodore doesn't 'go under'.

But it did. I watched the TV in shock as the entire population of Theodore climbed into helicopters and was airlifted to safety as the town went under.

I caught glimpses of familiar faces and buildings I knew so well. People gathered outside the art deco pub where I had my first official beer on my eighteenth. The choppers landed on the grassy traffic islands of The Boulevard, the landmark water tower visible behind them in the main roundabout of town. (Theodore was originally planned by Walter Burley Griffin — yes, the very same one that planned Canberra — and the large traffic islands and many roundabouts in the tiny town are his legacy.)

I was relieved to be asked by the ABC to 'help out' with the emergency coverage

Previous page: Some St George locals went to extreme lengths to save their homes. This house escaped inundation thanks to levee banks built around its entire perimeter.

Right: Central Queensland's rail links were severed by the floods and tracks were heavily damaged.

in Queensland. While I knew my family was physically safe, there was just no way I could focus on my work in Lismore, where I am based, while their community and others around them were leaving their businesses and homes to the floodwaters that just seemed to keep coming. At least I would be in Queensland doing what I could do best for people: getting information to them and getting their stories out to others.

Initially I drove to Toowoomba, to work out of the Southern Queensland ABC studio. My partner, Rob, was based there so I was able to be with him. Toowoomba was a good option logistically as it was close to some of the worst-affected communities, and, unlike Rockhampton, it was accessible. It was also safely located at the top of the Toowoomba Range, so in no danger of flooding. Or so we thought.

It's hard to describe the day that Toowoomba was hit. I wasn't even in the centre of town when it happened. Rob had presented breakfast and I was on a day off. We knew the rain was coming down pretty hard because despite his ground-floor flat being located at Mount Lofty (one of the highest points in Toowoomba), it had started to flood. We pulled the furniture into the centre of the room and picked the piles of books off the floor and put them on to the table.

With his gear safe and nowhere to sit, we headed into town to catch a movie. We never got to the movie.

As we got closer to the centre of town we realised something wasn't right. There was water everywhere; parks were awash; big pieces of bitumen were sitting in the grass beside the road like icing peeled off a cake; we saw cars with debris wrapped around their tyres piled up against each other. And then we saw some swift water rescue guys in their yellow overalls running down along the churning creek with torches and ropes. Realisation washed over me and I said to Rob, 'My god, they're looking for someone.'

Rockhampton's Fitzroy Hotel, nicknamed 'Fitzroy Float-el' by owner Tony Higgins, becomes the local watering hole in more ways than one.

The next week was something of a blur. The rain just kept falling. That same storm caused the flash flooding in the Lockyer Valley; the water carried away cars, houses and people. The road down the range was closed and for a couple of days not even the authorities could get into the Lockyer Valley.

It was all hands on deck: we got the local programs to air and they were just hours of weather and flood warnings, evacuation orders, emergency information and callers letting us know what was happening where they were. At that stage those callers were often our only source of information about some of the smaller communities. We also had calls from listeners looking for family and friends from the badly hit towns of Withcott, Grantham, Gatton and Murphys Creek. One of the joys of working for the ABC is being able to give people the information and news they are looking for. But this time we just didn't have the information to give them. I took one of those calls and when I hung up, I had to wipe away my tears before I took the next one.

When I left Toowoomba, a week after the flash flooding, it was still a town in shock. People would stop at the bridge that crossed East Creek in the centre of town and look down in silence at the trickle it had once again become. I took my dog for a walk before we left and when she stopped to cool her belly in the little stream of water, a couple nearby looked down at us with concern apparent in their faces, as though the water might just turn up again with the same speed and ferocity as the last time.

From Toowoomba I travelled to Rockhampton where I was working as part of the ABC's flood recovery team. I was paired with Rachel Fountain, a 'Rocky' girl who was working for the ABC in Western Australia. The Rockhampton airport was closed so we flew into Gladstone and hit the road.

Our role was to ensure we were getting to recovering communities to hear, and to help them tell, their stories.

Above: People pitch in any way they can – baker Charlie Fuller came to Theodore from Brisbane to help feed those affected by the floods.

Opposite: Police in wetsuits and lifejackets wade along a flooded street in Depot Hill.

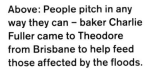

We visited communities across the region including The Caves, Rossmoya, Yaamba, Wowan, Depot Hill, Lakes Creek, Bluff, Comet, Blackwater, Emerald, Springsure, Rolleston, Woorabinda and Duaringa.

Given what people had been through and the huge task that lay ahead, I wasn't sure people would want to talk to us and I would have completely understood that.

But I needn't have worried. People were exhausted from shovelling mud, from sweeping and scrubbing, from lifting couches and fridges, but they still shared their stories. They showed us through their water-marked houses and their mud-smothered communities, they cried as they told us of their fears for themselves, their families, their businesses and their communities. And they laughed too. I stood with Diane in front of her Depot Hill house as her rotting frangipani trees were removed from her garden with the stinking mud. She told me, 'Laughing makes it a bit easier.'

Stories of small kindnesses were everywhere: furniture lifted, meals cooked and animals rescued by neighbours, friends and strangers.

Steve, a dairy farmer, was out repairing the road with his kids because the council was 'pretty stretched'. Colin, a sweet potato grower, pulled his spuds through 4 km of floodwater with a modified tractor to get them to the markets where they were needed. Glen, Helen and their tenant Therese had never met each other until they had to clean out their inundated house and in three exhausting days they became close friends. Reg and Denise had put their retirement fund into a business that was now swamped; their insurance did not cover flooding. A work crew from the local prison known as 'The Farm' was working to restore Rockhampton's waterfront. One of the men told me, 'It's nice to have people smile and say thank you instead of the usual frown.'

The resilience of people has astounded me and I've begun to think that perhaps it is times like this that people are at their best. Some of those walls we

South-west of
Rockhampton,
the filthy expanse
of water appears
endless.

build between each other seem to have crumbled; it has been a time of looking out for one another and experiencing something together.

Don't get me wrong, this is no fairytale. While it would be nice to wrap up with a happy ending, that would not reflect the horrors many have gone through. It's been an exhausting and devastating time. There are people, businesses, families and communities, like my hometown of Theodore, who will never go back to how things were.

But it seems that there are already people recognising the opportunities in that.

Some in Theodore were already planning to rebuild, bigger and better, as the choppers flew them to safety. Some, on returning, spent weeks helping others reclaim their homes, lives and businesses from the mud and water. All the while, ideas flew back and forth over the internet as the community brainstormed how they could create something positive from this terrible event and come through stronger and more vibrant than before.

I know now that I underestimated the power of nature. Thankfully, I also underestimated the capacity of people to keep going in the face of hardship.

Water will flow on, mud can be removed and buildings can be rebuilt. I have learnt that communities are built on the spirit of their people.

Above: On 14 January, more than a week after the Fitzroy River peaked, Roy Bennett must wait longer still for the water to recede from his home.

THE UNEXPECTED FLOOD

by Peter Gunders

ABC Cross Media Reporter based in Toowoomba

WE HAD BEEN ON FLOOD WATCH SINCE MID-DECEMBER. CHRISTMAS CAME AND WENT, AND WE KEPT WORKING, WATCHING LOCAL TOWNS INCLUDING DALBY, CHINCHILLA AND CONDAMINE ALL SUCCUMB TO THE SLOW CREEP OF FLOODWATERS.

And now the water was headed west. So that's where we went, to report on what experts were promising would be a record flood.

By Monday 10 January, people in St George and Dirranbandi were breathing a sigh of relief. The Balonne River didn't hit the expected peak, and particularly for St George, a town that had experienced two '100-year floods' in less than twelve months, it was good news. If you can call a major flood that still wiped out crops and inundated a number of homes 'good news'. But it could have been much worse.

When the waters stopped rising, and the fear of disaster abated, our stories started to focus on things other than water level watch. People fishing from park benches that weren't usually so close to the river's edge became news.

Then the radio came to life.

We were staying at the same motel as the swift water rescue team. Luckily, they

Left: The entire population of Condamine was evacuated when the Condamine River burst its banks twice in a fortnight.

Below: When Dirranbandi in southern Queensland was cut off by rising waters, locals say that the flood markers became popular meeting places.

weren't very busy. I remember talking to them over breakfast at a café, and wished them a boring stay in St George. If there's one group of people you can wish to be bored during a flood, it's these blokes. It means no-one is in trouble in floodwaters.

But there were people in trouble. Just not here.

'I think they said Toowoomba,' someone commented.

Toowoomba? My town? I reasoned it must be kids messing around on body boards in one of the small creeks. That happens when it rains in the city on top of the Great Dividing Range.

While I was covering the floods out west, talking to people preparing for floodwaters to hit, I was asked on more than one occasion, 'How's your place, Pete?' 'Oh, I'm fine, I live on top of a mountain,' I would reply. 'If Toowoomba floods we'll all be in strife.' We'd have a chuckle and then get back to talking about real issues. It was a 'fact': Toowoomba was one place that didn't have to worry about a flood.

But something was amiss on 10 January. It was time to get home.

Above: Local schools presented a brave face to their communities, despite the flood.

Like all good media vehicles ours has a police scanner, and even though we were hours away from the drama in Toowoomba, it came to life with news from those in the thick of the disaster.

We kept heading east, hoping the roads wouldn't be closed (almost half of the state was flooding and while the Balonne had peaked, other rivers were rising), all the while listening to the situation in my hometown play out through the police radio.

The next morning a fog lingered over the centre of Toowoomba; teamed with a

Above: The levee in Dirranbandi helped keep floodwaters out of town. It was monitored during the floods, and any leaks were pointed out with red markers to be 'plugged'.

chorus of beeping bobcats and tow trucks performing under their flashing amber lights, it made for a surreal experience. We all knew Toowoomba didn't flood, yet here we were standing in a street that had been submerged. The creek might have been almost back to normal, but nothing else was.

This flood crashed into people's lives. Literally. The people I interviewed over the coming days all had amazing tales of survival. The flood was so fast and furious, yet so localised, a few metres meant a world of difference.

Days later I was chatting to a firefighter. He wasn't on duty when the flood hit, as his shift started later that night and he was home looking after his children. He told me of his own struggle that day, wishing he was there to do what he was trained for, to do his part for his community. I knew how he felt.

This was a flood no-one expected, in a place no-one expected would flood. There was no time to prepare. No time to fill sandbags, to move property, to brace for it. But it didn't take long for the community to rally. Everyone was involved now.

I struck up a conversation with a bloke standing behind the bar at the Murphys Creek Tavern. His name was Troy. He was quick to tell me about the people who needed help, and how the tavern had become the central meeting place for the townspeople, the place to collect donated goods that had arrived from all over the country. 'Our house got destroyed, yeah,' he said matter-of-factly when conversation turned to his own plight. After helping his wife and three-year-old onto the roof, he didn't have time to climb up himself, so he clung on to the verandah for forty minutes as floodwaters rushed through his home, dragging away everything he owned. He took me to his house and showed me where he hung on for his life.

'Mate, I saw shipping containers, halves of houses, cars, fences, trailers, fridges – you name it, it went past me.'

Every now and then a tear would well up in his eye as he remembered that forty minutes of 'hell'. He told me there were two things that raced through his mind while he clung on to the back verandah. First was, 'Am I going to survive?' And then he repeated the second thought to me just like he did to himself: 'Don't let go. Do not let go! Just hang on for grim death, mate, you will survive.'

He did survive, and so did his sense of purpose and humour. 'I'll rebuild in the same spot. Except I won't build a low-set, I'll build a high-set!'

A flash flood in a city no-one thought could ever flood? A wall of water a few minutes later in the valley? Troy in Murphys Creek summed it up best: 'One minute we were dry, the next we were drowning.'

Above: Murphys Creek resident Troy Johns shows where he clung for his life on his verandah.

Opposite: Murphys Creek locals send out a message of gratitude.

Left: A truck trailer in Murphys Creek has collapsed in on itself.

Below left: Roadside piles of rubbish signify the beginning of a long and difficult clean-up in Murphys Creek.

Below right: Floodwaters washed away cars and dumped them at Murphys Creek.

Right: This is all that remains of a house in the Lockyer Valley. The rest of the building was washed off its foundations.

IT WOULD NEVER HAPPEN TO ME

by Jenny Brennen

Local Radio Manager for 612 ABC Brisbane and Queensland

IT'S JUST STUFF. I DON'T KNOW HOW MANY TIMES I HAVE HEARD THOSE WORDS COME FROM MY MOUTH OVER THE PAST FEW DAYS.

Days that are fast blurring into a melange of murky, adrenaline-soaked images, as if I'm walking through a movie starring me as me.

In my ten years working for ABC Local Radio I have produced and overseen a number of emergency broadcasts. Fires in Sydney's northern suburbs, flooding in Victoria's Gippsland region, the odd cyclone or two and countless storms and flash flooding have honed my skills at helping to build prepared and resilient communities. But a week ago when it became apparent that maybe, just maybe, I might find myself part of the story, I thought it would never happen.

Last Monday we were in our usual routine of briefings from key agencies and the weather bureau as we entered the third week of broadcasting to a flood-ravaged state. Our focus, as always, was ensuring that those Queensland communities at risk of flood were kept informed and prepared. So what happened a few hours later was at first unbelievable and then simply shocking.

We stood around our TVs watching Toowoomba being swallowed by a furious cauldron. 'What just happened?' we asked ourselves. As quickly as the waters surged

Right: It's just stuff – a sentiment echoed by many to ease the sense of loss. In Fairfield, Brisbane, someone's belongings are piled on the footpath for collection.

through the town, it became evident that lives had changed forever. In those few minutes all bets were off – that water was going somewhere and we all knew where.

Staff scrambled to keep on top of the unfolding events – we were now providing rolling coverage to listeners in southern Queensland as people tried to grapple with their fear, disbelief and the slowly growing death toll. By darkness we knew the next twenty-four hours would be somehow different. Science was starting to crack under the weight of random events. That dreaded year 1974 crept into the vernacular as the city of Brisbane inched closer to something we thought would never happen again.

And still it would never happen to me.

The house I lived in was built along a dip in the road in the low-lying riverside suburb of Graceville. 'Mind the dip,' the road sign screamed at cars as they drove along a street crammed with poincianas that muffled the sound of endless home renovations. This dip was now posing a major threat to our little suburban life.

On Tuesday morning I insisted to my partner that we commence the arduous task of bringing everything from under the house onto our verandah. Maybe it might just lick at the floorboards and we'll be okay, I thought to myself. The Zen master finally conceded that maybe, just maybe, such a step was needed and got going. As the rain saturated the city, the kid disappeared into his virtual Xbox world as dad hauled dozens of boxes of stuff up to a place we hoped would be high and dry. Meanwhile I was back at the office feeling uneasy and unsure – I wanted to keep the panic at bay but it just kept nudging me until finally I relented.

At 11.00 a.m. I went back to the house. I needed to get my family out of there. The rain was relentless, as if it needed to hammer the point home that this wasn't just your average rain event but something more sinister. As I drove across the Indooroopilly Bridge, my dreamlike state began. Water covered the vast area of the Graceville netball courts and as I watched them slowly fade into the background, I knew it was serious and there was very little time left.

Opposite: Clotheslines indicate the extraordinary level of the floodwaters as they continue to encroach upon Depot Hill, Rockhampton, on 4 January.

At the house my Zen guru had moved mountains. I started flinging clothes onto top bunks and tried to make rational decisions about what we may need for a few days. I couldn't let myself think that it may be more than that. Get passports, photos, birth certificates, insurance or whatever the hell you are meant to do. Somehow in all the years of educating our audience on emergency preparedness, I had neglected to prepare my family for such an event. The house was starting to resemble a jumble sale. The stuff was piling up to the roof.

The following days merged into a flurry of activity. Waiting for the peak and then spending days not knowing what may await us was a surreal experience. Local Radio relocated to the Gold Coast for a few days so that we could keep broadcasting to the Brisbane community after our phone system in Toowong fell over. These were days spent in blissful ignorance of my own situation as work gave me all the distraction I needed. I knew it couldn't last.

I asked the Zen master to be the first to return to the house. He would report back on the Friday, and then come Saturday morning I would commence the task of cleaning up and assessing the future.

The drive back to Brisbane with my colleagues was long. What seemed to be the whole of South-east Queensland was mobilising to help the 'victims' of one of this country's worst natural disasters. Crossing the Indooroopilly Bridge, I breathed deeply as I braced myself for what may be on the other side. All of us went silent as the enormity of the situation became all too apparent.

There was stuff everywhere. Traffic jams of cars, people and more stuff. An army of optimistic helpers descended on homes to help the dazed and confused. The real army blocked off streets and washed roads. Pulling up to my house, I was gobsmacked. The sound of generators and gurneys (water sprayers) became the soundtrack for a day that will live with me for a very long time. A day when strange women washed all our mud-soaked crockery. When men drilled holes through

Right: A West End resident watches the debris floating in flooded Ryan Street.

Above: Residents
of Burrendah Road,
Jindalee, watch on as
a bobcat clears away
their belongings.

Opposite: Steps lead
into the hazardous
floodwaters in Bundaberg.

the floors to help the stinking brown sludge wash below, and little kids pushed a river of water out of our house.

I delegated tasks and watched the transformation begin. Ladies from suburbs far away took clothes to wash, dry and fold; one brave soul insisted that my record collection was worth salvaging and has taken on that challenge. Others have offered assistance of all kinds and there are plans for a flood street party once the power is restored. It will be a party of tears washed down by the good fortune of a community that helped each other jump a wall that at times seemed almost too big, too daunting and very dark.

Our future is uncertain. We don't know if we will ever be able to live in our house again and certainly not in the short term. So a new minimalist life awaits us – a life that has changed as we learn to live without the stuff. It may just be stuff, but it was our stuff. Precious pieces of a journey so far and a life lived. Pieces that sit piled to the sky in the memory heaps that now dot our suburban parks, awaiting their final destination. For the moment they serve as shrines to what we have lost but more importantly to what we still have – our memories and ourselves. It's just stuff.

AN UNFAMILIAR HOMECOMING

by Lisa Millar

ABC's North America Correspondent based in Washington DC

A QUEENSLANDER WHO GREW UP IN GYMPIE, LISA WAS HOME FROM THE UNITED STATES FOR THE CHRISTMAS HOLIDAYS WITH HER FAMILY WHEN THE FLOODS HIT.

It is 2.30 a.m. and I'm driving through Brisbane's hilly streets. From the television towers of Mt Coot-tha to Spring Hill, past the strip clubs I reported on decades ago as a young journalist, across the Story Bridge where I kissed an old boyfriend, to Kangaroo Point where my colleagues are waiting.

This route is locked in my brain. A producer and I planned it just hours ago on the phone. At each intersection I plot it again. Should I turn left here instead? Will taking that side street avoid trouble? Will Fortitude Valley flood if the city centre does? I worry I've missed something, a trap, a dip in the road where the water will silently surge toward me.

Slow. That's how I'm travelling. The city is dark. Traffic lights work sporadically and the streets are empty except for a couple of police cars that seem to dawdle past me. My mind drifts back to a time when I worked as the early morning reporter on the now-defunct *The Sun* newspaper. The paper's offices were in the

On the night before power to
the CBD was cut, the serenity
of this scene belies the
ferocity of the Brisbane River
as it swelled to its peak.

Valley, when being there at 3 a.m. meant you were either drunk or a prostitute. Or a journalist. And here I am again. In the Valley at 3 a.m. Twenty-one years later. I'm in my mother's car, not mine. I don't even own a car. To me this feels like a foreign country. I'm driving on the wrong side of the road. This isn't home. But it is. This is my home. And the river that runs through it is just hours away from wrecking thousands of lives.

Let me backtrack.

As a foreign correspondent for the ABC you ask a lot of your family and friends. You ask them to sacrifice time away from you, to worry when you dart off into dangerous places, you ask them to understand that an aunty, a sister or a daughter is not there when they need help. A child is born, a friend marries, a friend dies, parents move into a retirement village and you are missing in action. So eighteen months into my second posting in the ABC's Washington bureau and having already missed one family Christmas in Australia, I fly into a muggy Brisbane, landing on 25 December at 7.45 a.m.

It is raining. And it seems to never stop.

Waking each morning at my parent's new retirement home, the first sound I hear is angry pelting from the sky, water pouring into a makeshift drain my 85-year-old father has made so my mother's new garden won't drown. And then I hear the television. I lie there feeling selfishly robbed of a summer holiday back home as ABC News 24 relays the latest rainfall figures, the rising of the rivers, the homes swamped in Rockhampton, then Theodore, then Emerald. A French friend in DC rings to tell me French TV is reporting the waters cover an area the size of his country and Germany combined. I know, I tell him. I am here.

I check in with friends producing the bulletins in Brisbane. Would they like me to come in? I'm happy to. I feel bad I'm not helping. Reporter friends on television look exhausted and there is still so much more to do. No, no, they say.

Left: A car driving through Brisbane's West End sends up a spray of floodwater.

You're on holidays. You're with your family. Don't come to work.

By now, we're at a beach house on the Sunshine Coast – my sisters and a brother, their children and my parents. It's a family reunion of sorts, a week that's been a year in the planning.

We sit glued to the television.

We watch flash floods in Toowoomba, the devastation in Grantham; phone calls come in from old family friends whose farms have been ruined. School friends email photos of the tennis courts at Woolooga where I used to play junior fixtures, now under water. And we share the sinking acknowledgement that this is so much bigger, so much more devastating, than anyone had ever imagined.

'Good bulletin last night,' I text to TV producer Fiona Crawford on Wednesday 12 January. 'Can you call? Sydney wants you on deck' is the response seconds later.

Below: Toowoomba's famous Queens Park sustained significant damage.

Opposite: Cash registers and a bar sign from the National Hotel in Toowoomba have been washed into a nearby street.

It's a funny thing — the relationship between the ABC and the Millar family. We are 'country Queensland' people. We still think of ourselves that way despite leaving the farm at Kilkivan long ago. The ABC was the only source of information worth trusting, the only form of entertainment worth watching. To have a member of the clan working for the ABC, becoming a foreign correspondent, is a source of pride.

But when I tell them I'm going to work, the disappointment is heavy. 'Aunty Lisa, can you swim in the pool with me first? Pleeese?' five-year-old Eva asks.

We're not sure if I can even make it down to Brisbane. The road is cut at Caboolture and the water is playing games with us. Up one minute, down the next. My brother Bob, whom we'd forced to take a holiday, is already back at work. He's a councillor for the Moreton Bay Regional Council and has returned to chair the Local Disaster Management Group. The locals there have had 600 mm of rain in three days.

The Bruce Highway is clogged with traffic. I stop to fuel up and the service station owner nods to the queue of cars waiting for space at the bowsers and says, 'They're all going to Brisbane to see if they can save their houses. They should stay away if you ask me. I hope you've got a good reason for going.'

Right: Sandbags are in place at the Port Office Hotel, Brisbane city, to hold back the approaching floodwaters.

Left: Wheelie bins make it through the flood in St Lucia, a Brisbane suburb bordered by the river on three sides.

Below: Tables and chairs from exclusive waterfront restaurants at Brisbane's Eagle Street Pier join the wreckage.

I head to the Red Cross evacuation centre at the RNA Showgrounds in Brisbane. Hundreds of people are already coming in the door, deposited by council buses that empty their load then turn around to go back for more. The passengers bring their children, their pets, a favourite pillow and wear their anxiety like an anchor around their necks.

It is quiet here apart from the children. The volunteers have them laughing and singing in a corner of the cavernous exhibition hall. It's now evening and I'm doing live crosses in the middle of the crowd while they stand and watch me on a large television screen in the corner. I'm relaying stories that people have told me about their grief and their loss as they watch their private fears made public.

A tired mother sighs when I ask how she has come to be here. She moved to a hostel in West End from North Queensland just a few months ago. She is trying to start her life over. The police told her to leave the hostel and seek safety. Now she's

On 11 January, the Brisbane River surges over the Regatta Ferry Terminal in Toowong.

clutching two children and a blanket. A third child – a teenage boy – sits slumped in a plastic chair, listening to music, ignoring this latest upheaval in his life.

A Chinese woman in her thirties sits with her forehead resting on a fold-up table. She was in her fourth floor apartment when the waters started rising. She's a visiting student at the university with no idea what to expect. She shakes her head in disbelief and is longing for home. Not her St Lucia apartment but the safety of Beijing.

The scene is surreal. I feel like an intruder.

I head to the home of my friends, Karyn and Gerard, near Mt Coot-tha. They know I have to be awake in a few hours to report for ABC News 24 from the cliffs at Kangaroo Point as the river reaches its peak.

Karyn has been warned I have to raid her wardrobe. My holiday luggage of swimsuits and T-shirts won't cut it for live television the next morning.

It's late now and she has nothing that fits.

Above left: A pontoon in Brisbane's CBD struggles to keep afloat on the swollen river.

This page: A ferry terminal pontoon is inundated at Eagle Street Pier in Brisbane's CBD.

She asks if I remember her friend Renaye, who hosted her baby shower.

I do.

She tells me Renaye's Yeronga home is about to go under. She and her husband filled their car with what they could save and left it in Karyn's garage. Birth certificates, passports, laptops and … Renaye's clothes. 'Maybe we could go through her suitcases?' Karyn tentatively suggests.

Hours later I'm standing in front of a camera in the dark of the early morning, wearing a jacket belonging to a woman whose life has been turned upside down. It feels macabre but somehow appropriate.

The questions from Melbourne come in one ear. The other is listening to the sound of the water.

I thought the river would be powerful but silent. It is loud. And furious. Ferry pontoons, truck tyres, concrete slabs are racing past me. The river is roaring out its intention to wreak damage: it's demanding our attention and fear.

The numbers swirl around as fast as the water. It'll be 5.5 metres, they say. No, it's 4.9. Then 4.6. Each estimate of the peak offers another centimetre of hope.

As 4 a.m. arrives we know the river is not going to reach the heights first thought. It is a lower peak but thousands of homes and businesses are now under water.

Even so, there is a sense of relief among the sightseers who've turned up. They're now more excited about the politicians who are here before the cameras. Tony Abbott arrives, then Kevin Rudd. The crowd takes photos of them and ignores the mass of water in front of us.

I'm thinking of Renaye and the jacket I'm wearing. And of the one life among so many who will have to start anew. And of the river that rages through the city I call home.

EVERYONE HAS A STORY

by Spencer Howson

Presenter of *Breakfast* on 612 ABC Brisbane

EVERYONE IN BRISBANE HAS A 2011 FLOOD STORY. EVEN IF YOUR OWN HOME REMAINED DRY.

I overheard someone say that flood stories are like dreams. You really don't want to hear other people's.

There may be some truth to that but, as with dreams, we need to share them with someone else. You can't keep them bottled inside.

I'm going to tell you mine.

I was on summer holidays, at home in Indooroopilly, when the phone rang and I was called back to work. The Brisbane floods were still two weeks away but Central Queensland was under water and it was decided we needed a local, Queensland New Year's Eve program.

A talkback caller suggested it was a good thing 2010 was behind us. My response was cautious: I remember saying that this weather event has not finished with us yet and for some of us, 2011 will in fact be worse. I wish I'd been wrong.

Ten days later, on Monday 10 January, I had decided it was time to enter the digital TV age at our house, so I was out purchasing a set-top box. A quick check

Right: On Saturday 15 January, Gareth Sheard sorts through the damage at his Milton workplace.

SINGLE
RCA -
VIDEO

of Twitter at the shops and my attention was drawn to a series of photos posted on the 4BC website. Photos of extraordinary flooding in Toowoomba, at the top of the Great Divide, a ninety-minute drive west of Brisbane.

I came home. My sister-in-law Carly, who was flying to the UK on Wednesday, had arrived from Toowoomba moments earlier. She had just received a call from her sister Anthea, who was stuck in her car in Toowoomba with water up to the doors. I plugged in the new set-top box and went straight to ABC News 24. They were showing footage of cars surfing along roads. We couldn't believe it.

Carly rang Anthea again. She was okay: the car had ended up wedged against a fence. How very lucky.

Carly had just driven down from Toowoomba, down the range, through towns that were about to make headlines around the world: Withcott, Gatton and the like. If she'd set off two hours later, she may not have made it.

Left: A car is left wrapped around a tree in Withcott, a township located at the bottom of the Great Dividing Range.

Above: The tilted 'Welcome to Withcott' sign indicates the direction from which the wall of water roared into town.

By dinnertime that day, I was hearing unofficial reports of thirty deaths in the Lockyer Valley and Toowoomba. My wife Nikki, a television producer, had been recalled from holidays, with one-hour news bulletins being planned for the rest of the week. I was called in to work overnight on the radio.

Unable to verify the death toll, but aware of the credibility of the information, I went on air at 10 p.m. suggesting – in a line we would hear repeatedly from our Premier – that we must steel ourselves for bad news.

I told producer Amanda Dell what I'd heard about the death toll. For a moment, we stopped and looked at each other, both of us tearing up. We busied ourselves to regain control.

That Monday night, Brisbane City Council announced 220-odd properties in the state capital would go under as a result of the water coming down from Toowoomba. Almost

Below: The town of Grantham was declared a crime scene in the wake of the flood as police conducted a house-by-house search for bodies.

cruelly, the council could only give suburb names and the number of properties in each. Nothing more than that. More specific information would be on the council website in the morning.

Being school holidays and with Nikki back at work, I was spending my days at home maintaining normality with our ten-year-old son Jack. We weren't going to flood at our house, although flash flooding could cut us off.

Another sister-in-law from Toowoomba, Dee, and her fiancée, Pete, were holidaying on the Gold Coast. They wouldn't be able to get home after what Police Commissioner Bob Atkinson called the 'inland tsunami' had come through the day before. So they diverted to Brisbane and set up camp with us. Eventually we would end up with twelve people under our roof, instead of the usual three. Dee

Above: Rubbish and debris line Fig Tree Pocket Road in Brisbane's south-west.

and Pete bought a boot-load of groceries on the Gold Coast, supplies that I deemed unnecessary – 'you didn't have to' – but that would prove invaluable as the days unfolded.

On the Tuesday, council issued a list of streets expected to flood. I rang a friend in Fig Tree Pocket to say his street was on the list and to offer help. Dee, Pete and I would go over straight away. He said to call the next morning.

Wednesday morning, first thing, I rang him again. 'We have to come now,' I said. 'Or we won't get in.' His reply: 'It's too late. I'm already stranded.'

By now the game was changing rapidly. Authorities were warning of a 'worse than 1974' flood to peak at 4 a.m. on Thursday. The city tensed.

Carly was to fly from Brisbane to London at 11 p.m. When we heard the news that all public transport would be winding back from Wednesday lunchtime, and unsure what roads would be impassable, we set off to drop Carly at Eagle Junction train station, the last station on the Airtrain before Brisbane Airport. To get there we devised our own ring road around the west and north of the city, up to Stafford then across to Clayfield

and Eagle Junction. Later we learned we had done well. By then, we wouldn't have made it through any other way. Poor Carly was twelve hours early for her flight, but she was at the airport.

Near Eagle Junction, council buses were being parked, one after another. We noticed trains stationary and in long lines on high parts of the Ipswich rail line. The city continued to brace itself.

We'd been warned 100,000 homes would have their power switched off as a safety precaution. Not being on a low-lying street, we never expected it would include our place. But it did. I went out in search of ice but there was nowhere selling it within half an hour's drive, so I headed home and switched on the battery-powered digital radio.

We'd heeded the request on the radio not to go sightseeing. But by Wednesday afternoon, something told me we needed to see to believe and to understand. Dee, Pete, Jack and I joined onlookers on the rooftop car park of a shopping centre near the river. Then we went to Sylvan Road, near the historic Regatta Hotel. Water was well past the hotel, up the street and under a rail bridge. Nearby Memorial Park was a lake. Kayakers were fetching essentials like medicine for residents unable to get into their homes. And several dozen people stood watching the water creep along the bitumen.

That night I was back at work by 9 p.m. with the flood peak expected at four the next morning.

By this stage we were playing the cyclone siren on 612, something quite unfamiliar to Brisbane listeners, but bringing back terrible memories for anyone who had lived further north.

On air from eleven until five on Thursday morning, I quickly gained the sense that much of Brisbane couldn't sleep. And much of the world was with us, holding our hand. We started receiving messages and phone calls from all over the world, including Canada, London, Switzerland and South America.

There were three items of concern in the river that night: our only remaining vehicular ferry, the Moggill Ferry; a former ferry turned nightclub called The Island; and a floating concrete walkway, which ran for several hundred metres along the river. There was talk of scuttling one or all for fear of them breaking loose and causing damage downstream, especially to the Sir Leo Hielscher or Gateway Bridges.

The Moggill Ferry hung on and our party boat survived. It was our floating boardwalk that decided to become a floating battering ram.

As the chunks of concrete headed for the Gateway Bridge pylons, the remarkable news came through on Twitter that we had our own Bruce Willis, a tugboat operator who had nudged the boardwalk off its course. He hadn't saved the Earth from a meteor but he had prevented a collision with the Gateway Bridges and the M1 high above.

Throughout the night, the Bureau of Meteorology downgraded its estimated flood peak. First it was dropped 30 cm to 5.2 metres, then 'under 5 metres'. Of course, each centimetre would save more homes. As it turned out, the Brisbane River peaked just before 3 a.m. at 4.6 metres, well below 1974 levels, but no less destructive or disruptive for those directly affected.

At 4 a.m., I went back to Sylvan Road in Toowong and described live-to-air the crowds still standing there, silently watching the water.

Opposite: A battered chunk of the floating Riverwalk comes to rest on Nudgee Beach after breaking free from its moorings in Brisbane city.

Left: On 13 January, with the Brisbane River at its peak, Milton residents look on as a boat is rowed down Blaxland Street.

Below: Green Hill Reservoir in Brisbane's Chapel Hill becomes a temporary dumping ground.

When I got home Jack was awake, so we went for a drive. I'd shared the floods with our listeners all night. Now it was time to share this event with my son.

We looked at complete roads under water in Chelmer and Chapel Hill, joining other sightseers. Again, there wasn't much talking. People just stood and looked.

I'm writing this exactly two weeks later. Dee and Pete made it home to Toowoomba. Nikki's aunty from Sinnamon Park, without power for several days, moved in. Then out again. And now our life has returned to normal.

But traces of the flood are everywhere still. There are clumps of washed-up vegetation in trees and fences. There are piles of spoiled possessions in parks waiting for collection. And there's no movement whatsoever on the river – our thriving commuter ferries have been sidelined, many of the terminals washed away.

But the overwhelming feeling I have right now is of disconnection. Because we didn't go sightseeing to the worst suburbs, because we didn't have power for a day (no TV or internet), because our newsagent couldn't deliver papers for a week, I am still amazed by every image I see of my city under water. It's like it happened to another city, yet I know it's my own Brisbane that's been punished this way.

That's my flood story. Whenever you're ready, come over for a cup of tea and tell me yours. I'm here and ready to listen.

Below: Water silently creeps up Coronation Drive, one of Brisbane's major arterial roads.

centre
of destruction

STORIES FROM CENTRAL QUEENSLAND

by Alice Roberts

Cross Media Reporter for ABC Capricornia

THE LANDSCAPE IN CENTRAL QUEENSLAND HAS CHANGED VASTLY IN THE LAST 18 MONTHS: FROM THE RADIANT RED DIRT OF DROUGHT TO THE BLACKENED HILLS OF BUSHFIRES, AND FINALLY TO THE FLATTENED LAND OF THE FLOODS.

As floodwaters inundated homes in Rockhampton, Emerald, Theodore and small communities in the region, I flew home to Rockhampton before the floodwaters covered the tarmac.

What shocked me most flying over the city was the sheer amount of water surrounding it. I couldn't even make out the usual landmarks; it was just an endless expanse of water.

There was no indication that the Capricorn Highway, the road from Rockhampton to Emerald, ever lay there except for the odd sign poking up above the water. 'Road subject to flooding' signs reaching out of the brown murk almost seemed humorous.

But there was nothing to laugh at here.

Listening to the stories of those at the evacuation centres was heartbreaking.

Above: A bobcat pushes sludge off the road.

Previous page: A 'Welcome to Rockhampton' sign appears less convivial when partly submerged.

ROAD SUBJECT TO
FLOODING
INDICATORS SHOW DEPTH

A road sign near the swollen Yeppen Crossing, Rockhampton, seems grossly understated.

Old Bridge, which spans the Fitzroy River to connect north and south Rockhampton, crosses raging floodwaters at their peak on 5 January.

Above : Rockhampton evacuees John Peacock and Anthony Scully outside the evacuation centre set up at Central Queensland University.

I met Rockhampton resident John Peacock, whose description of the floodwaters rising in his home was so vivid it gave me goose bumps.

He evacuated after hearing the sounds of his children's Christmas presents banging up against the doors downstairs, swimming in a sea of muddy water and a pit of snakes. And while he lost most of his belongings, all he would say was there were others worse off.

Time and time again we would hear those same words from others who had seen footage of the floods down south. But that didn't take away from the emotion experienced by individuals or whole communities here.

Emerald resident Ginny has lost everything. All she managed to save was a few items of clothing for her children, their Christmas gifts and some camping gear. They are living on Ginny's in-law's couch, with nine people, two cats and two dogs in the small home. She says they're hoping to have their home up and running as quickly as possible.

'Well I have to, this is all I've got,' she says. 'This is our home, we haven't got money to just go and buy somewhere else.

'My kids' dad died seven months ago so it's just me and the kids – so we can't go anywhere else.

'We have to try and fix up what we've got and at the moment it's got no walls, it's got no floors in places, no power, no nothing. It's still our home, but it's a shell of our home.

'Eventually we'll fix it up.'

One gentleman from Theodore described the aftermath of the floods as being like a funeral. He said there's a huge amount of support for people in the beginning, but it won't be until weeks or even months down the track that the emotion will sink in and they'll have to deal with it on their own.

During the floods I had the opportunity to head up in the ABC helicopter to see a different perspective of the water on the outskirts of Rockhampton.

While I was high up in the air and pumped with adrenaline, I was quickly brought back to earth by the sight of one couple. Their house, now an island, stood defiant in the murky depths. They sat on their verandah as if it was all so natural. No doubt luckier than some, as the water lapped at their top step.

Many in Rockhampton too chose to stay. One man, Eric Dare, thought of himself as the caretaker of the homes in his street that lay empty.

'I can spotlight up this street, down this street, down there and there,' he says. 'But the police are very good; they come around every thirty or forty minutes.'

One group of people who will continue to feel the effects of the flood for many years to come are the farmers. I travelled out to Theodore soon after the recovery had begun and met with cotton grower Trevor Brownlie.

He says he lost 90 per cent of his March crop due to floods, 100 per cent of his crops this year and it won't be until March of 2012 that he'll be able to cash in his next harvest. For most the idea of two to three years without an income would be unthinkable.

As we spoke with him he walked through what little remained of his beaten crop. Just dried twigs, once worth thousands of dollars, now not even worth the shirt on his back.

'But we'll pull through; I think most blokes have a positive attitude, a ready to go type of thing,' says Trevor. 'But mental health will be a problem: maybe in two weeks' time, when people sit down and start looking at what happened and where do we go from here.

Above: Rockhampton local Eric Dare patrolled in his boat to keep the homes in his deserted street safe from looters.

On 2 January, three days before the Fitzroy River reached its peak, floodwaters have already inundated historic Quay Street in Rockhampton.

Opposite: The extent and severity of flooding in the Lakes Creek area of Rockhampton is apparent from the air.

Above: SES volunteer John Rasmussen helps to transfer emergency staff and medical patients between Rockhampton and Gracemere, which were separated by floodwaters.

Above right: A man rides his bike through floodwaters in East Street, Rockhampton.

'At the moment everyone's so busy helping each other they haven't got time to think of their own problems.'

But despite the overwhelming sense of loss, pride shone through. Trevor's son Ryan spent hours clearing out sheds and helping to put things back in some sort of order. Trevor says he never knew his son could work so hard and was beaming with pride.

But the attitude out there is 'you get on with it' and that's exactly what those in Central Queensland are doing. As we find ourselves on the other side of some of the worst floods in Australia's history, the community has pulled together to give their neighbour, friend or a stranger a helping hand.

Just talking to one another is helping these small communities piece together some form of normality. For many, 'normal' is many years away, but the rebuilding and healing of the community is taking steps toward recovery daily.

And if it's shown us anything, it's how resilient, stoic and strong the people of Central Queensland really are.

GRANTHAM

by Paul Lockyer

Senior Reporter, ABC TV News and Current Affairs

AS WE EDGED OUR WAY IN THE ABC HELICOPTER AROUND THE THUNDERSTORMS AND THE SHEET LIGHTNING CLOAKING THE GREAT DIVIDING RANGE WEST OF BRISBANE, THE FULL SCALE OF THE DISASTER THAT HAD STRUCK THE LOCKYER VALLEY WAS SUDDENLY REVEALED.

Through the rolling cloud and the driving rain emerged a scene of utter devastation, framed in the eerie light of a grey dawn. This was where the small town of Grantham once stretched out along the banks of Sandy Creek — a creek that seldom carried more than a trickle through the settlement. But on that fateful afternoon of Monday 10 January — as a deluge sparked a dramatic flash flood through the centre of the nearby city of Toowoomba — the same downpour generated a torrent that swept down the Lockyer Valley to the east. The terrified people of Grantham had little or no warning as the deadly wall of water bore down on them.

The wild weather did not ease and throughout the night that followed there were only sketchy reports about what had happened in the Lockyer Valley. Forty people had been winched to safety from the floodwaters by rescue helicopters late on the

Right: The flash flood left Grantham devastated and reeling.

afternoon of the disaster but as night fell there were grave concerns for entire communities dotted through the valley.

The weather grounded helicopters over much of South-east Queensland. We had attempted to get to the Lockyer Valley from Toowoomba after the flash flood hit the city but were blocked by the bad weather. We spent the night at Dalby, further west, determined to strike out at first light for Grantham. ABC chopper pilot Gary Ticehurst carefully negotiated a course through the thunderclouds and the rain, and there below us were the remnants of the town.

As camera operator Berge Breiland captured the first aerial images of the destruction, Gary and I peered through the gloom looking for signs of life. There were none. We began to fear the worst. All we could see was massive devastation on a scale normally associated with a severe cyclone rather than a flood. Building after building reduced to rubble. Some homes plucked from their foundations and carried up to a kilometre away to be dumped in the middle of a paddock. The incongruous sight of cars, boats and even planes slammed into buildings or swept into treetops.

The railway bridge that crossed Sandy Creek played its own lethal part in the disaster. It became a barricade against the torrent. Vehicles, with people still clinging to them, smashed into the bridge or were sucked under the metal structure. Later, eighteen vehicles were recovered from the wreckage around the bridge along with refrigerators, washing machines, television sets, household furniture, shipping containers and parts of houses.

Only at first light on Tuesday 11 January was all this

Below: Twisted car wrecks are among the carnage in Grantham.

Opposite: Police tape on a tree is a grim reminder of the ongoing rescue and police work in Murphys Creek.

becoming evident. We landed in the ravaged main street of Grantham, near the hotel, which had been all but destroyed when a concrete tank had been swept up in the floodwaters like a cork and slammed into the building.

Out of the wreckage of the town a survivor finally emerged. Kel Wood's story was to become all too familiar by the time the day was done. 'What happened here?' I asked. 'Armageddon,' came the reply. Kel told us how he, like many others in Grantham, scrambled onto a rooftop as the torrent consumed the town, and waited for hours in the rain for the water to drop far enough for them to try to get to safety. As people clung for dear life to houses, trees, power poles or anything they could grab, they saw others being swept past and heard the cries of anguish from those trapped in cars and houses. Kel Wood was finally overcome with emotion when he pointed to the wreckage of a home near the pub. He knew the people who lived there had no chance of getting out.

As we filmed at the centre of the destruction, the water running through the town began rising again. We quickly moved the chopper to high ground, where we found the survivors of Grantham sheltering in the small school. By chance there was a police officer in town. He wasn't stationed there but was married to the school principal and this was his home. He provided leadership at the evacuation centre. A generator was found to provide power, and townspeople who had escaped the torrent rallied around to organise food, clothing and blankets.

Shock takes different forms. Some survivors wept, comforted by others. Some sat in stunned silence. Others wanted to talk. Dramatic accounts of survival and rescue unfolded.

Rob Wilkin was on a nearby farm when the flash flood came. He managed to drive two workers to high ground in his ute – then got into his boat and saved another four people before the vessel ran aground on the railway line. He and the others then ran for their lives down the railway tracks with the torrent lapping at their heels.

As Norrie Blume was watching the water rise, he saw a four-wheel drive vehicle being swept towards the railway bridge with a young woman clinging to the roof. He fought his way through the water to the middle of the bridge; just before the vehicle smashed into the structure, the woman leapt into his arms and he carried her to safety.

It wasn't until later that morning that rescue helicopters could start ferrying the survivors to a bigger evacuation centre nearby. But they would be the only choppers to move in the area for another twenty-four hours. We spent the day, and the night, bunking down with the survivors on the classroom floor – continually filing their stories to a wider world.

As Sandy Creek began to drop the next day, revealing even more devastation and debris, the survivors began to question how they had been spared when others had not. Some are determined to rebuild, others say they can't face it. The task is too big, the memories too harrowing. And they say that every time Sandy Creek starts running they'll be worried that it could herald another disaster.

Opposite: The army spent days searching in Grantham for missing people.

Below: In Grantham, a pulverised house is testament to the destructive force of the flash flood that tore through town.

THE GREAT FLOOD

by Richard Fidler

Presenter of *Afternoons* on 612 ABC Brisbane and *Conversations with Richard Fidler* on 612 ABC Brisbane, 702 ABC Sydney and 720 ABC Perth

Wednesday 12 January 2011

Today the Brisbane River has run over its banks and taken a few giant steps towards our building.

612 ABC Brisbane is in emergency broadcasting mode. After my shift I hiked up to the roof of the nearby Toowong Shopping Centre with some co-workers, where we can see the water creeping up Sylvan Road, putting the ground floor of the Regatta Hotel and several apartment towers under water. The area is eerily silent. Police have cordoned off the flooded section of Coronation Drive and there's virtually no traffic.

In the distance we can see two guys kayaking between the apartment blocks.

For the last four years 612 has been housed temporarily in the ground floor of a commercial building in Toowong. Right now we don't know whether we'll be in this place tomorrow, if the river rises as forecast. The decision whether to evacuate will be made around 4 a.m. tomorrow with the high tide. If we do have to get out, the plan is to set up at the evacuation centre at the RNA Showgrounds.

At South Bank the waters are swelling up onto the lawns in front of the Gallery of Modern Art and the State Library. The city shopping centres are closed up and the Riverside Expressway, a tangle of motorways propped up on towering concrete

Above: On Tuesday 11 January the Regatta Hotel, an iconic pub on Coronation Drive, Toowong, is sandbagged and cordoned off in preparation for the imminent flood.

Brisbane's much-loved Riverwalk floats in Moreton Bay.

pillars, is also now closed as the water rises underneath. This city looks strange to us and we tell each other that we'll remember this day for the rest of our lives.

There are stories that bands of complete strangers have assembled across Brisbane to help people move their precious belongings to higher ground before the high tide. In Fairfield someone called Ross showed up with a tip truck to offer help to a young couple. Some neighbours pitched in. At Rosalie the owner of the bike shop rushed into the supermarket and asked a queue of strangers for help, and all of them came to her aid.

Thursday 13 January 2011

I wake up at 4 a.m. to check on the high tide and hear Amanda Dell reporting from the river in Hamilton, where she and a group of onlookers saw a 300-metre stretch of New Farm's Riverwalk rush past on its way out to Moreton Bay.

At the 612 office there is relief: the river peaked lower than expected. We will not need to evacuate our Toowong studios. Across Brisbane the filthy floodwaters are forming huge pools and are starting to stink. Producer Scott Spark likens the smell to a damp camel.

Producer Anthony Frangi went to the river at dawn, where he met an elderly woman sitting on a bench, taking in the exact same scene she witnessed from the same bench in 1974. Then he saw another woman retrieve a book that had been washed up on the street. She found a name inscribed inside and went to track down its owner.

Rebecca Levingston has returned from broadcasting from the evacuation centre at the RNA Showgrounds. When the crew arrived at the centre at 4 a.m. they were wondering why it was all so quiet and apparently empty. Then they were directed behind a partition wall and saw in the darkened space seven hundred people asleep on air mattresses.

Above: The Brisbane River flows towards Coronation Drive and onlookers on Tuesday 11 January.

At Auchenflower, traffic signs are the only indication that the Bicentennial Bikeway exists beneath the swollen Brisbane River.

Left: Tow truck operators were busy after flash floods hit areas such as Toowoomba, retrieving cars swept away in the torrent.

Volunteers at the centre had set up an activity space for kids. Bec's eye was caught by the puzzle table, where she saw newly homeless people quietly sharing stories as they slowly tapped in the pieces of a thousand-piece jigsaw: a picture of a country cottage with manicured gardens.

I've just recorded an interview with Carol, our security officer here at 612. Carol's house is in East Ipswich. The waters rose up beyond her roof. She hasn't been home for days because she can't get through by road. Carol's been told her house now has a 'granny flat': a shipping container filled with timber that has come to rest on top of her carport. A water tank and a fridge have also drifted onto her property. She hasn't had much sleep, lying awake at night, dreading what will greet her when she goes home.

Tuesday 18 January 2011

An army of volunteers labours in sweet sunshine across the city, mucking out houses, apartments and businesses. Uncannily, the fine weather arrived at the same time as the floodwaters and has been with us for a week; it's the longest stretch of fine weather Brisbane has enjoyed since the La Niña effect began. But small isolated thunderstorms are rolling in this afternoon.

I'm still getting used to the drama of a Brisbane storm: the first sign is a brace of clouds with a metallic, greenish tinge at the edges, followed by the crash of thunder and then a drenching downpour falling from a turbulent sky.

Brisbane's summer skies often look like they have two completely different cloud systems super-imposed on each other; sheets and puffs of cloud seem to intersect at odd angles.

Last year I interviewed two storm chasers: photographers who actually seek out big storms and race to good vantage points. They choose to live in Brisbane because its geography and proximity to particular oceanic and atmospheric currents make it one of the planet's major storm centres.

You have to think hard to remember that just years ago Brisbane was in severe drought and seemingly perpetual sunshine, and we wondered what we'd do if Brisbane ran dry. My daughter was four years old then and I used to quip, 'Emma thinks the internet is normal, and rain is weird.'

During today's program, ABC reporter Matt Wordsworth calls in from Grantham in the Lockyer Valley, where people are being allowed to return to

Above: Clean-up volunteers stop for food and drink that has been prepared and distributed by another band of volunteers.

their homes. Yesterday the names of the deceased and missing were posted at Grantham's little primary school. The locals have asked the media to leave for the rest of the week so they can grieve in privacy.

Reports are coming from Ipswich this morning of price gouging: three kilos of bacon on sale for $45, a loaf of bread for $10. Ipswich Mayor Pisasale's response on Madonna King's program this morning was a classic: 'We've got a long memory in Ipswich. And I'm sure these shops are now going to need a lot of roadworks right in front of them for the next ten years. To me they are "un-Ipswich".'

I've never heard the phrase 'un-Ipswich' before.

Carol, the 612 security officer, is at work again today. She's been back to her house in East Ipswich. Just ten metres across the street from her are houses that are completely unaffected. Neighbours and relatives are rallying to help her. The 'granny flat' slid off and crashed onto two fences. The stray water tank has been claimed. No-one appears to want the waterlogged fridge.

The afternoon storm has passed over our office and the rain is starting to abate. Another line of storms is on the way.

Right: Thick, oozing mud is scraped off the pavement in West End, one of Brisbane's oldest suburbs.

TWO WEEKS IN IPSWICH

by Rhianna Patrick

Presenter and Producer of *Speaking Out*, ABC Local Radio

ABOUT A 40-MINUTE DRIVE SOUTH-WEST OF BRISBANE LIES IPSWICH, QUEENSLAND'S OLDEST PROVINCIAL CITY.

It is home to the state's first secondary school and at one stage it was in the running to be Queensland's capital. The flooded city had received little media coverage and a fraction of the number of volunteers that had helped Brisbane the previous weekend, so I was prepared for the residents to greet my colleague Brett and I with a 'bugger off' response.

What I found was a city trying to come to terms with what had happened. And what I wasn't prepared for was the effect the next two weeks would have on me.

The CBD of Ipswich could have been renamed the 'lakes district' after the nearby Bremer River rose to 19.5 metres and engulfed the centre of town. Brett spoke to a woman who'd lost her business on the main drag, Brisbane Street. She was standing in the shell of what was left of her shop, telling him about how overwhelmed she was by the generosity of Queenslanders. One phone call that particularly touched her was from a man whose late wife had been a beautician. In the three years that she'd been gone, he'd never quite managed to let go of all her leftover stock or equipment. He was more than willing to drop off what he had if it would make a difference in rebuilding

The 'We Care' Aboriginal and Torres Strait Islander Service for Aged Care and Disability in the hard-hit suburb of North Booval.

her business. She cried while re-telling this story and couldn't believe that this stranger was willing to part with his wife's former possessions.

I've read and heard a lot of people talk about the smell of the mud that was left behind by both the Brisbane and Bremer Rivers. By the time I got to Ipswich, it wasn't so much the smell of mud but the smell of a giant garbage tip. It was this smell that greeted us when we drove into North Booval, a suburb that backs onto the Bremer River.

I couldn't believe what I was seeing; it was something out of a movie – too surreal to comprehend. We saw houses with their fronts completely washed away and their contents spewing out onto what was left of the footpath. As we made our way around the streets, the rubbish on the kerb started to tower over the four-wheel drive we were in. We turned the corner and ran into army troops trying to clear piles of rubbish that used to be the contents of a family home.

It was hot, 35 degrees or so, and all you could smell was baking garbage. It started to get harder to see the names on street signs as the piles climbed higher and wider. What should have been two-way streets could now barely fit one car down the middle.

Above: Rhianna Patrick with Brett at Wivenhoe Pocket, which was isolated by floodwaters for a week.

We finally made it to Helen Street, where an Indigenous organisation had gone under. While Uncle Eddie took me inside what was left of the two-storey building, Brett went across the street to chat to one of their neighbours. Uncle Eddie wasn't sure how long the rebuild would take or how they were going to continue looking after their clients.

Each community or suburb we visited welcomed us warmly. Many were happy to share their stories so others would know what they were going through. Jeff, the owner of a townhouse in Brassall, was at his lowest ebb before the local rugby league team,

Above: Glamorgan's community fire shed, which was pushed across the road by a torrent of water – with the fire truck inside.

the Ipswich Jets, dropped by and cleaned his house in a matter of hours – a job he had been working on for four days without making a dent. He told me if they hadn't arrived when they did, he would have given up.

We visited the communities out the back of Ipswich in the Brisbane Valley, places like Lowood and Fernvale, where the navy had been sent to help. Locals at the Glamorgan Vale Hotel told me about watching the community fire shed get pushed from one side of the road to the other with the foundations still intact. It was a week later when I was told that the fire truck was still inside.

What broke me was meeting an 82-year-old woman from Patrick Estate, which was hit hard by the water let out of Wivenhoe Dam. She took me down on the back of her tractor to her home and showed me where the water got to a metre high in her two-storey house. 'It makes me want to cry,' she told me. 'But what can I do? You've just got to get on with it.' She reminded me of my late grandmother and I cried.

But there were stories of hope too. Wivenhoe Pocket was cut off for a week by floodwaters and in that time the residents organised themselves into a mini council. They briefed locals twice a day about what was happening and what needed doing. They cleaned out twenty-five flooded houses and found billets for those who needed a place to stay. One of the residents, Otis, said he was proud that his daughters were learning what it meant to be a part of their community. And then there were the barbershop guys in Goodna, who had lost their shop but not their spirit. They set up their remaining equipment on the footpath and got back to cutting people's hair.

It was a hard two weeks but I'm grateful to those people who opened up their lives and shared their stories with me. It's something I'll never forget and may never experience again.

a community of
heroes

FLOODED WITH KINDNESS

by Madonna King

Presenter of *Mornings* on 612 ABC Brisbane

JADE. GLEN. HANNAH. ON PAPER THEY'RE JUST NAMES, NAMES YOU MIGHT HAVE CONSIDERED CALLING YOUR CHILD OR THE NAME OF YOUR DAUGHTER'S BEST FRIEND.

In Queensland, in January, they became so much more. Each of them told a story, one that's difficult to describe without feeling the torment behind the water torrent that swept across the state without discrimination.

Jade is just eight, but she made her parents drive 100 km to give her new pink bike to someone she didn't know, because they'd lost their toys in the water that engulfed the Brisbane suburb of Oxley.

Glen lives downstream from Oxley. He got out early. He couldn't afford not to, not with three young children and the youngest with a serious medical condition.

But it was the image of him the next day that I won't forget. He struggled through water that climbed up to his chin, to find his home and his future destroyed. I read it on his face and just wanted to hug him.

Hannah lives a couple of hours up the road in Toowoomba — not that addresses matter much when a torrent of waters surges indiscriminately on a reckless path,

Previous page: SES teams in Grantham took part in the tragic search for missing people.

Right: Swollen rivers across the state threatened to engulf the structures that traverse them.

levelling millionaires' homes and rural sheds, destroying the dreams of the young and the old, and leaving behind orphans, widows and widowers.

Hannah was anonymous for a couple of hours. Police released an image of her, a dot in a muddy, angry river of water that turned Toowoomba on its head, with a plea to find her.

It didn't take long. The same community spirit that flooded donation lines led police to the young woman who will live with her harrowing fears long after most have forgotten them.

Her rescuers were a couple of blokes you might not look twice at in your local pub. Today they're holding their heads high as heroes.

Larry and his men should too. Night and day, as waters climbed buildings and snaked into homes, they took to helicopters and boats and trees and roofs and pulled those they could from the angry waters that threatened to swallow them as well.

Some of them had big wins, saving entire families. Others today are still wondering if they could have done more, if they could have saved just one more child.

That's what happens when whole families disappear in a couple of seconds. Some grabbed for a phone, to warn loved ones what was happening. It was better to know, than to wonder.

That selflessness is a bit hard to fathom for the rest of us. But it showed itself over and over again — not least in the case of Jordan Rice, a 13-year-old who, despite a fear of water, told rescuers to save his little brother first.

At his funeral, his big brother Chris told how he used to tease Jordan, or 'Weedsy'.

'You were so shy, always hanging off mum. You were petrified of water, heights

Above: The 2011 floods may influence how councils zone residential land in the future.

This shopping centre's underground car park is filled with the overflow from a large drain.

Left: Driving around flooded towns and cities became a complicated operation when hundreds of roads were cut by rising waters.

Opposite: Cleaning up is a heartbreaking time for people who must discard their former precious possessions.

and even the dark. How wrong was I? Here you go losing your life from one of your biggest fears to save your little brother. You made me so proud. What you did took heart, courage and love.'

Stories like Jordan's have turned suburban streets into civilian army camps. A call to arms one weekend saw thousands and thousands of mums and dads march down streets, carrying mops and buckets, and wearing big smiles.

They walked into homes they'd never noticed before and started scrubbing. They shovelled silt 10 cm deep from stairs and removed dead fish from pantries, helped take lounge chairs from backyard swimming pools and left at the end of the day wanting to know when they could come back.

You don't mess with a school fete convener, and mums like Karen Simons, along with local parents and citizens' groups, ran suburb-wide operations from their kitchens.

Karen didn't have power and she didn't even know most of the people calling her house their temporary home. But as news spread of her generosity, everyone from

soldiers to the homeless dropped in for a cold water, a home-made sandwich, even a listening ear.

Karen will have her own demons to confront. Knowing that waters were engulfing her friend's home, she grabbed a kayak and took to the streets, guiding it around corners, past parks, and through the front door of Anne's house.

Anne, like so many others, lost nearly everything, but that doesn't really matter. It's just her daughter's room that makes her hurt. Her little one didn't know when I spoke to her, but her pink bedroom was lying out on the footpath. All four walls.

Heartache followed heartache for so many families. After cleaning their home, even using toothbrushes to get the sludge from every nook and cranny, Anne and her husband were told the walls had to be demolished.

In many cases, that unleashed another beast. Along footpaths, asbestos sheeting lay discarded. In the urgency of the moment, long-term worries were laid aside. That's a problem for another day.

Down the track, people will think of what comes next: whether we want the same relationship with our river, whether a home on the river bank is a sign of success or a shadow over your shoulder, whether we need to re-look at how our communities grow and how our land is zoned.

The cost of those few Christmas holiday weeks is hard to fathom. That's a debate for another time too.

But it's the community spirit that has floated to the surface in the end: an indomitable spirit that has carried the army of volunteers to their next job, that has local communities of company directors and concreters and accountants working for the local fete convener. It's the spirit of young people like Jade, an eight-year-old whose heart is so big she gave away her shiny pink bike to another little girl she's never met, but whose smile will not be drowned by the torrent of tears that flooded Queensland in December–January 2011.

EMERALD RISING

by Craig Zonca

Presenter of *Regional Drive* on ABC Local Radio Queensland

IT'S NEW YEAR'S EVE IN EMERALD AND THE RISING SUN'S REFLECTION FLICKERS BRIGHTLY IN THE FAST-FLOWING NOGOA RIVER. 'TODAY'S MY BIRTHDAY,' BRAD TELLS ME.

Brad was told to pack up and leave his home twenty-four hours earlier. Water had already entered his yard as he backed out of his driveway. Now, it's an anxious waiting game for the brown, murky floodwaters to recede. Brad has no idea when he'll be able to return to his house, or what he'll find. An army Black Hawk helicopter flies overhead; tonight there won't be any celebratory drinks.

At the council chambers, men and women in uniform are manning the phones —you catch snippets of ten different conversations. They are tasking supply drops, sending out swift water rescue teams and hurriedly arranging the evacuation of a number of expectant mums. Although you'd expect chaos at such a time, there's a sense of calm.

The Mayor, Peter Maguire, waves me into his office. 'We think it's peaked,' he says. The latest reading has the river at 16.05 metres, its highest level on record. The rising floodwaters have forced hundreds of locals to leave their homes. Almost 500

Right: Waters encroach on Emerald's residential streets. Hundreds of residents sought refuge in evacuation centres.

are staying in evacuation centres; many more are rolling out swags on the lounge room floors of family or friends.

The Mayor has a camp bed sitting in the corner of his office but the exhausted look on his face suggests he hasn't had a chance to use it. His blood-shot, tired eyes tell the story – the flood is devastating for this town and those that surround it, he feels the pain of the residents who have lost their homes and businesses, and realises the magnitude of the job ahead to rebuild Emerald.

Back outside I follow the constant stream of 'Emeraldites' walking east along Clermont Street. Road closed signs, traffic controllers and a couple of police stop us

Above: A cyclist makes his way through floodwaters on Morse Street, Emerald.

Opposite: Emerald was isolated when the airport was cut off from the main township.

about 500 metres from where the river bank would normally be: today water is lapping close to our feet. In front of us the Vince Lester Bridge, the main access across the river, is 1.5 metres under water. The gathered crowd is wide-eyed as they marvel at

the force of the water. Like the town, some families are split in two, with mum and dad on the west and their children and grandchildren on the other side of the raging torrent. An enterprising helicopter company has a sign advertising their services for those who want to get across; it's not a cheap exercise.

Talking to locals snapping pictures with their digital cameras, you hear of a great sense of frustration, even anger. It was only at the start of 2008 that the Nogoa River was at a similar height. That flood was supposed to be a one in a hundred year event. This one is worse. 'It's bad, really bad,' one tearful local says.

Less than a month ago, Maurie and his wife Connie hung new front doors on their house as the final chapter of rebuilding after the last major flood. I remember being at their house almost three years ago to the day. Back then, Maurie told of fish left flapping around on their back patio as the water receded while friends helped to hose, wash and disinfect every room. This time they built a mezzanine floor in the shed to store their furniture and other possessions higher than before. Unfortunately, they fear that won't be high enough. It's a cruel blow.

We sit down for a cuppa and hear that Maurie is now known as 'Captain Pugwash', to signify his role as the self-appointed ferry commander for Selma

Road. Feeling the emotional torture of not knowing the true extent of the damage they'll face, Maurie reflects on the strength needed to recover: 'I just wish I didn't have to put Connie through this again … it's bloody tough … but we'll get by.'

John's home is a little further down the road from Maurie's. Three years ago, water had reached the ridge capping on his roof. This time, there's not a dry area on his entire block and the house is fully submerged. Just like in 2008, John was quick to make sure his dogs, Guinness and Kilkenny, were in the ute ready to be first out. He tells me with a sly smile that there's a gas-powered fridge where he's currently staying – at least I know where to go for a cold beer. It'll be another five days before he'll be able to get back to the place he calls home.

As the New Year breaks, the water slowly recedes and the clean-up begins. Two weeks ago, the residents of Kidd Street were celebrating a win in the community Christmas lights competition. Rope lights spell out 'Season's Greetings' and reindeer-shaped frames covered with fairy lights are still on rooftops, but the power is off at every house. Piles of filthy mattresses, swollen doors, mud-covered electrical appliances and children's toys litter the footpath and inside many homes the gyprock has been stripped from their walls. It's at such a time you see what resilience and community spirit really mean.

The street is clogged with cars. Friends and family of those affected fill their utes with gurneys (high-pressure sprayers), mops, disinfectant and gumboots. Local mine workers start the heavy lifting and backbreaking washing at one end of the street and progressively make their way along. Stopping in at Peter's place, we both struggle to hold back tears as he describes how friends have helped to clean up the sludge that covered almost every surface: 'I'll never be able to repay them.' He laughs at the suggestion that having a drowned lawnmower should get him out of the chore for a few weeks.

Opposite: Shops and businesses in Emerald were hard hit; this stranded shopping trolley tells the story.

Opposite: The army helps to cart out tonnes of wreckage and waste.

Above: SES crews provided invaluable assistance throughout the duration of the floods.

Despite the mud and debris, everyone I speak to talks of hope, that things will be okay. Mother Nature has not been kind to the people of Emerald, but she will not deter their spirit or attitude. As new friendships are formed and neighbours get back to having their weekly barbeques, the question of how to say thanks has an easy answer in a town like this: an icy cold beer should do the trick. And if you want to know how to help, put Emerald on your list of places to visit, spend a dollar or two and stop for a chat. It's a town that won't be forgotten.

Left: The massive
clean-up begins – a
volunteer sweeps out
sludge from a house.

Above: Many small
businesses have suffered
in the floods but the loyal
support of patrons can help
them to recover.

CITY OF MUD

by Simon Marnie

Presenter of *Weekends* on 702 ABC Sydney

THE PLANE TIPPED TO ONE SIDE AS WE PREPARED TO LAND IN BRISBANE ON SUNDAY, THE WEEKEND AFTER THE FLOODWATERS PEAKED IN QUEENSLAND'S CAPITAL.

I looked out the plane window, my eyes captured by a vast mud plain. The dark red dirt stretched as far as I could see and was seared by white 4WD tracks that ran in evenly spaced parallel lines. I thought back and tried to remember such a mud flat on Brisbane's surrounds but couldn't place it. Then it slowly dawned on me: this was no mud plain, they were not dirt tracks — I was gazing down at Moreton Bay and the etched lines were waves.

As my taxi wound its way to the city, I began to wonder just how bad the floods were. It was the same summery city I'd seen in past years, with masses of road construction and new buildings overshadowing the classic Queenslander houses perched on poles and resisting the incessant heat and march of progress.

When we hit the Brisbane River suburbs I started to get an inkling of what was to come. It wasn't the pontoon rammed up against the bank on the other side of the river, nor the plastic water tank suspended high in the mangroves in Hamilton; no, what gave it away was the smell. There was that muddy, mouldy, messy smell in the air, a

Right: Floodwaters besiege Brisbane's iconic floating restaurant Drift, moored on the western bank of the Brisbane River in Milton.

bit like old socks, a lot like a house with rising damp where wafts of mildew combined with the aroma of rotting bananas and off milk. Over the next few days I'd get them all: fermenting grapes, festering fruit and rotting rubbish would characterise each suburb in the way a winemaker might describe a vintage.

From then on I'd get used to seeing total devastation, only to drive 50 metres up the road and find a suburb serene in its survival. Such were the twists and turns of the Brisbane River, what destroyed one part of a street spared another. The only facet of the flood that didn't respect boundaries was the smell — it wafted across the roads where the water couldn't.

The next day we drove in the early hours though the low-lying suburbs of Graceville and Rocklea. Imagine a council collection in your local area. Imagine every household has put everything they owned onto the footpath for collection. Imagine the footpath isn't big enough to hold those discarded possessions; they link up so in the end you have one long thread of waste that goes the whole block, from gutter to gate, tall enough to block the view of the front yard. Imagine that wall of waste runs along each side of the street and then imagine someone has come along with a huge hose and sprayed the wall of waste with thick congealed mud. That was Oxley Road, Graceville. A sign propped on a corner pleaded for compassion; it said, 'Beep to Show u Care'.

Below: Residents call on support from passers-by. Whole communities came together to comfort and help one another.

Opposite: Gardens that were once proudly tended sink beneath the waters.

From Graceville to Brisbane City Markets in Rocklea. Through roadblocks and police cordons, past huge trucks entering and leaving the once-bustling hub of fruit and veg for the city. The shops in front of the market look like they've

been looted, with fridges turned over, and chairs and tables tangled in a mash of mess. Behind the shops the market is preparing for its first day, the marketeers desperate to return much-needed fresh produce to city shop shelves left empty when people stocked up ahead of the flood.

Again, the smell. I asked one worker if there was a piggery nearby; he laughed.

But the scene of greatest devastation was still to come. Goodna is one of those suburbs on the urban fringe, a mix of rural land fighting back the city, and a city fighting its way into farmland. It's also where the Brisbane River snakes in a huge U before winding its way down to the big city. I imagine in better days it's an idyllic little place that savours its riverside location.

The first sign something is very wrong is the small bridge over Woogaroo Creek.

Below left: Destroyed produce and stock is shovelled onto the kerbside at Rosalie Village in inner Brisbane.

Opposite: On 13 January, sandbagged shops at Merthyr Village, New Farm, are spared from flooding.

The railings are mud-covered, with trees and matted vegetation woven into the fence. We're on a dirt road, thick and slippery; there is no kerb where the guttering should be. The local service station is deep in mud, the bowsers surrounded by black dirt, at least a foot thick. Opposite is the Goodna RSL Function Centre where the sign still advertises Weddings, Parties, Corporate Meetings, Anything.

A hundred metres down the road the car park for the Goodna Aquatic Centre has become a makeshift depot for emergency vehicles and earthmoving equipment. There's a high-water mark on the centre's roof just a metre from its very top.

Jim Runham, a Navy Cadet Commander from Ipswich, tells me that his boat sailed over the top of the Aquatic Centre's roof as they battled currents of up to 20 knots (40 kilometres per hour). Jim reckons they did fifty-six rescues across the week: 'Fifty-six rescues, one dog, one cat and a one-legged chicken; there were gas cylinders, cars and shipping containers floating past.' Now he's joined at the Aquatic Centre by sixty-odd volunteers, who are emptying the swimming pool – pumping the water out first and then removing the thick soup of sludge bucket by bucket.

As army trucks trundle by and helicopters pass overhead, I wind my way back to the RSL. There'll be no weddings, parties or corporate functions there any time soon. The waters from the river less than fifty metres away have rushed through the front doors and swept up all the contents. Next door at the bowling club it's even worse. Inside it looks like the most vindictive vandals have wreaked the worst possible destruction. Most of the contents – the trophy boards, the chairs, even the ceiling – lie in a mound beside the car park. All that remains inside are a dozen poker machines lying in a tumbled heap.

Outside, the treasured bowling greens are an exception to the rule. From early morning volunteers, assisted by the greenkeeper, have painstakingly removed the 20 cm of mud that covered each green and are now raking what has become newly deposited topsoil in a smooth layer. Two older women members who call themselves the 'Mud Queens' are stoically determined to get life back to as normal as possible as soon as possible. One Mud Queen tells me, 'We're not going to give up. We were 'sposed to play this Saturday but we don't want to push our greenkeeper too hard.'

But it was Jim Runham who captured the mood best. He ran up to me as we were about to leave. 'I gotta tell you this story. We pulled this family of three out, a medical emergency, and we got 'em back on to safe land. They were new

Australians, been in Australia four years. One of them says, "Where we came from, a million people would die".'

Jim's tired; he gets emotional, which I gather is rare for this bloke. He grabs my arm, urgently. 'I tell ya,' Jim says, speech faltering, 'that really touched me ... that people care. That's what Australia is all about, people care.'

Opposite: In one of many such operations, an SES crew rescues local workers.

Above: A pile of sodden belongings outside a house waits to be cleared.

Right: A sign forbidding cycling and other wheeled activities on this footpath seems redundant now.

DIVIDED BUT UNITED

by Emma Sykes

Cross Media Reporter for 612 ABC Brisbane

I IMAGINE THAT PARTS OF THE THIRD WORLD LOOK LIKE MANY BRISBANE SUBURBS DID IN THE AFTERMATH OF THE FLOODS.

In the many flood-affected streets, muddied belongings that once filled homes were being stacked and thrown onto endless piles at the kerbside. Destination – landfill.

And yet 500 metres away in a neighbouring suburban street, houses remained untouched, high and dry in every sense of the word. I think that's what got me in the beginning: the fact that a natural weather phenomenon could strike anywhere, and that the difference between those affected and those not could be measured in centimetres.

It has always filled me with a frightening sense of excitement. I grew up in northern New South Wales, where some heavy rain could turn a calm creek into a swollen chasm overnight, and severe weather is a part of life. When you live in this part of the world, I guess you develop a memorandum of understanding about the forces of nature. But these floodwaters have left a muddy stain, both physically and emotionally, on residents across most of Queensland.

The scale of the onslaught was, as Premier Anna Bligh put it, 'unprecedented'. And yet the unmistakable generosity of spirit and the indelible Australian ethos of

Dam releases from Wivenhoe Dam, late afternoon on 19 January 2011.

Left: By nightfall of 11
January, the Bicentennial
Bikeway is steadily
disappearing beneath the
rising river.

helping out your mate in hard times burned so brightly for the world to see.

With almost half of Queensland already under water and a 'one in a hundred years' flood predicted for Brisbane and Ipswich, perhaps only those who lived through the 1974 flood knew what to expect. And even then, with things changing so fast throughout the unfolding disaster, all bets were off.

My role in covering the Brisbane floods was unlike anything I've experienced in my career to date. In a nauseating way, it's what a journalist lives for. The rush of information that was flowing from the emergency agencies almost as fast as water was being released from the Wivenhoe Dam, the breaking developments, and witnessing Mother Nature at her most ferocious. But the adrenaline soon wears thin and all that you are left with is the sinking feeling that tomorrow you'll wake to a changed city … and change the city did.

For some it changed just a little, for others substantially; many families continue to count the cost for them personally. For some residents, it will simply mean changing their routine – a neighbour won't be able to have her hair cut at her favourite salon in New Farm because it was inundated; friends who relied on the ferry services will now have to depend on other modes of public transport. But for most Brisbane residents the surreal vision of their city being swallowed by the strength and power of a river in flood; the smell of mud; the instant rubbish tips across Brisbane's streets; the unprecedented images of families being cared for in emergency evacuation centres across the city – these memories might just stay with them for a long time to come.

In a two steps forward, one step back kind of way, the people of Brisbane became more unified through this disaster even as they were being segregated by it.

Of the 150 Brisbane suburbs, sixty-seven suffered major damage, resulting in what most closely resembled a post-war zone. Residents of suburbs affected by the 1974 floods were advised that the flooding could cause their properties to be inundated again. Miraculously some of these suburbs were spared, but only by a narrow margin.

People came with cars, utes, trucks and, at the eleventh hour, boats to help neighbours, friends and perfect strangers retrieve whatever treasured possessions they could from their homes just hours before floodwaters would reach the ceilings. Some only just managed to get out in enough time to find a road to higher ground that hadn't been cut by the floodwaters.

When the floodwaters did recede, the sheer volume of flotsam deposited in and around Moreton Bay and along the Brisbane River told the story. Floating restaurants and riverside walkways had been plucked from their moorings; what once were expensive boats now bobbed on the river, battered and untethered, presenting additional safety challenges for authorities; Rocklea Markets, once the hub of the city's fruit and vegetable supply, was completely inundated and its produce floated far and wide.

A layer of mud and sludge covered the low-lying suburbs so thickly that only an army of volunteers could clean up. And they came in droves.

By the first weekend of the clean-up operation over 60,000 people had registered with the peak volunteering body, Volunteering Queensland. People were turned away from the volunteer coordination points across Brisbane because the response was so overwhelming. And those who couldn't clean up cooked up and hit the most affected streets to distribute food to workers and residents. Most would agree they've never eaten so well.

Thousands of Queenslanders are trying to recover from the worst natural disaster to affect the greater community in over thirty years. The rebuild effort will cost the economy dearly: early estimates put the bill into the billions of dollars.

Above: An evacuee makes her selection from the books on offer at a Brisbane evacuation centre.

Opposite: On 11 January, the Brisbane River bursts its banks and spills over the bikeway towards Coronation Drive. The waters will not peak for another two days.

Only now are the stories of the 2011 floods starting to be told. And now, more than ever, people are realising the power of community spirit and just how important it is.

There are some events in life that stop you dead in your tracks. They remove the blinkers from your eyes, let you see the big picture and remind you of the more important things in life. So the next time you're lamenting the trivial burdens of everyday life, spare a thought for those people who've swept their lives into the street with the mud, as they begin again.

Material possessions may have become a casualty in all of this, but memories have not. To those who have lost, remember fondly. To those fortunate enough to escape that loss, give generously.

Below: Milton Road – one of Brisbane's main arterials – has been reduced to a swamp at Auchenflower.

Right: The Fish Café on Brunswick Street, New Farm, succumbs to inundation.

TALES OF GILLAN STREET

by Scott Bevan

Author and Presenter/Reporter for ABC TV News & Current Affairs

KEVIN RUDD MAY HAVE ONE OF THE MOST RECOGNISABLE FACES IN AUSTRALIA, BUT AT FIRST I DON'T EVEN NOTICE HIM.

Perhaps it's because I have already had my fill of strange sights before reaching this moment, standing in water in Gillan Street.

Just a few minutes earlier, I had been on a bridge near the end of this street in the suburb of Norman Park, watching the symbols of ordered lives – household goods, boats, pontoons with chairs and sun umbrellas still attached – being ripped from all that is familiar and carried helplessly away by the destructive freeway that the Brisbane River has become. Mother Nature is turning the everyday into the surreal. Everything – and everyone – looks disturbingly out of place.

Finally, I recognise the gentleman wearing the ironically sky blue business shirt and rolled-up trousers, as he wades along Gillan Street, a riverside street in Rudd's constituency of Griffith. The renowned Rudd haircut is obscured by a suitcase balancing on his head, and water murkier than a factional brawl is licking his legs.

Back in 2007, before he was Prime Minister, Kevin Rudd stood before the Labor Party national conference and announced, 'My name is Kevin, I'm from Queensland, and I'm here to help.'

Right: A resident begins the arduous task of cleaning out his mud-filled home in Sherwood, Brisbane.

Almost four years later, on this clingingly humid Wednesday morning, Mr Rudd is knee-deep in giving those words new meaning.

The recently appointed Foreign Minister, who is also the local federal member, points to a house and explains it is rented by Korean students, but most of them are away. So he has turned up to give those still in there a hand in getting their possessions out. And with the water rising and creeping further along Gillan Street, Mr Rudd is determined to grasp another pair of helping hands.

Lord Byron, who was well versed in the art of escaping deep water, once warned, 'When we think we lead, we are most led.' Sure enough, just as I think I'm steering Kevin Rudd towards the idea of an interview, he is leading me into the water, towards the students' house. Before long, I feel the weight of knowledge bearing down on me: a suitcase containing books is tottering on my head.

As we push through the water, I'm breathing hard. The Minister somehow converts his breaths into words.

'The thing about the Brisbane River is, it's big,' he muses. 'People forget about it. Most of our capital cities aren't on huge rivers. This is. And when it gets angry, it gets angry.'

Once the cases have been off-loaded, we wade over to a block of units where the ground floor has already been inundated. Kevin Rudd stands next to a fence that comes up to our heads. 'This is where the 1974 floods came to,' he says, running his hand along the fence line. I think of the local newspaper's headline this morning, 'WORSE THAN 1974'. If this were tomorrow morning, when the peak is due, we could be in over our heads.

Mr Rudd notices an older bloke holding a can of beer and wearing neither a shirt nor, on his face, a care in the world. We meander over, and he introduces himself as Walter. The Foreign Minister asks if he's planning to evacuate. Walter replies there's no need, that his place is on the upper floor of the two-storey block of units

Above: The soaked and sagging remains of a kitchen in Fig Tree Pocket.

behind him, and that he'll be right. Kevin expresses concern that if this flood exceeds 1974, as is feared, Walter could get wet. Walter smiles beatifically and sips his beer.

'You've got to make me a promise, when I come back and knock on your door, you're gonna come out, alright?' the Minister orders.

'I've got a nice German schnapps and a beer for you,' Walter replies.

'Well, you've got to come out, okay? No stuffing around!'

Kevin Rudd is in no mood for stuffing around. He predicts that in his electorate of about 125,000 people, a quarter of his constituents could be flood-affected. So he is dashing off to another street in another suburb, West End, to see what can be done there.

Gillan Street continues to hum with activity and nervous anticipation, as residents load trailers and vans with the contents of their homes and lives. I notice a middle-aged man who had been helping the Foreign Minister earlier. He is still carrying bags and furniture, still helping whoever he can. I learn his name is Paul Hayes. To me, he will soon be 'Captain Paul'.

At any time other than during a flood, Gillan Street is blessed by its location. A cul-de-sac about 400 metres long, it is cradled in the crook of an elbow of Norman Creek, which enters the Brisbane River at the end of the street. So virtually every property in Gillan Street backs on to water. It's usually a marketing dream for real estate agents as a sign outside one house for sale attests, boasting of water frontage. Yet when the creek overflows, it means Gillan Street is gripped by pincers of water, and the blessing blooms into a curse.

By Thursday morning, there is no delineation between the creek, properties, and the road for about half of the street. It is one sheet of brown water. Still, the peak has passed, and the worst fears were not realised. A muddy line scrawled along fences indicates the water is already dropping.

The frantic energy of the previous day has been replaced by an unnerving stillness. The flotsam of proud households bobs listlessly at the end of the street. Residents cannot do much now except wade and wait.

While most feel helpless, Paul Hayes is still helping out by commanding a small dinghy. He's ferried a couple of neighbours who have evacuated but are returning for a look, overcome with worry about their home. He rows them along the canal that was yesterday their street. 'Captain Paul' offers to take me for a voyage. I offer to paddle.

We row to the home of Nadine Mammone. She stands, leaning over the picket fence, a portrait of domestic contentment. Yet the picture does not illustrate how Nadine is feeling. She, her husband and their two children have moved out to a friend's house on higher ground. Along with her mother, Judy, who is visiting from Victoria for a sunny Queensland holiday, Nadine has just returned to inspect their two-storey house. All of downstairs — her daughter's bedroom, a family room, the laundry — is inundated. A pile of sandbags leans pathetically against the laundry door.

Above: A piano records the high-water mark in a home in Fig Tree Pocket, Brisbane.

Still, Nadine utters something I will hear many times in the coming days.

'We are lucky compared to some,' she shrugs. 'You know, we've still got all our gear upstairs. And you just think of all those people in Toowoomba who had no warning, absolutely no warning, where we've had at least forty-eight hours to prepare.'

Across the road, a young woman is wading through waist-deep water towards her ground-floor unit. Her name is Ingrid Bailey, and for her, this is history repeating. In early 2010, she was flooded out in the western Queensland town of Charleville.

'So this is the second time in ten months,' Ingrid says, smiling unconvincingly.

She lives in the same block as Walter, the man who defied Kevin Rudd. I wonder how Walter is going.

Paul and I punt along the fences to his home, a beautiful traditional Queenslander perched on high stumps, majestically surveying the water all round it.

'It's your island and your castle,' I say to Paul, as we paddle through the front gates.

'I'm the Merchant of Venice!'

Paul explains he and his wife Vilma have just finished restoring the Queenslander. He raised the house to build in underneath, and the council insisted it be lifted 1.7 metres, much more than Paul wanted to because of the extra effort and expense. But now he is grateful, otherwise he would have water in the lower level of his home.

As we glide along, Captain Paul points out the mix of older, modest unit blocks, tastefully renovated Queenslanders, and contemporary, very expensive mansions. The many architectural faces reflect those who live in them, he says, ranging from well-do-to businesspeople and young families to tenants and university students.

The approaches in Gillan Street to combating Mother Nature are as varied as the residents themselves. One resident, a builder, has brought in pumps and an army of his employees to protect his large home. Meanwhile, Walter continues to employ benign indifference; we see him standing in the water as we paddle back towards the dry end of the street.

Walter tells me he has no regrets about ignoring Kevin Rudd and staying put. He reckons there had been 'scaremongering' about the water levels. Walter says he is now feeling very happy. He seems to be a 'glass half full' kind of character.

'It's nice and quiet, a carton of cold beer is in the fridge, half a bottle of German schnapps is still there, plenty of food to eat. Very happy,' he says. 'And there are people worse off than us.'

Optimism flows freely in Gillan Street, and as we row towards a power pole to tie up, Captain Paul is emitting sunshine about the future, even as storm clouds cluster above us.

The street will recover very quickly, he tells me.

'Yesterday, neighbours rallied around, going to low-set neighbours, asking did they want help moving furniture,' he says, 'and that's how it will be in the clean-up. We'll just hire some gurneys [water-spraying machines] and go from house to house, cleaning up.'

By the following morning, Paul's words are being realised. It's as though his sunny outlook has soaked up all the water in Gillan Street. The canal has been drained. A slick crust of silt covers the road and verges, but that will soon be peeled off and washed away by council crews, residents and volunteers.

Just over two days ago it was filled with water; now an extraordinary community spirit has flooded into Gillan Street. People are turning up with mops and buckets, shovels and a willing attitude. They don't say who they are or where they're from, but they're here to help.

I visit Ingrid Bailey's little unit. She's standing outside, looking at the ever-growing mound of mulch that is her possessions. She invites me inside, where a posse of helpers is hosing and sweeping the mud carpeting her floor. A huge, heartbreaking job lies ahead to return this to a home. Yet Ingrid is smiling with more conviction than yesterday: 'I came back [to Brisbane] for a fresh start. I got a fresh start!'

Ingrid introduces me to her boss and a couple of friends helping her clean up, but I wonder who the older couple is, sweeping in the lounge room. 'I actually don't know these two strangers over there,' Ingrid replies. I ask Ingrid how she feels about volunteers she doesn't know coming in to help her. That defiantly ever-present smile begins to tremble.

'I feel unworthy,' Ingrid replies, 'because I've had so many offers of support, and I do have people turning up all the time.'

The man, who introduces himself and his wife as Hugh and Robyn Somers from Manly, about 20 minutes' drive away, simply says, 'We're happy to help out.'

'We just feel so sorry for them,' Robyn adds. 'And we feel almost guilty that our house is safe, so it's the least we can do.'

All the way along Gillan Street, that attitude of 'it's the least we can do' is adding up to a whole lot of effort. Neighbours and strangers are shifting furniture back into homes, sandbags are being removed, and power crews are reconnecting electricity to some of the houses. Others will have to wait until their wiring has been checked and certified. But an electrician is volunteering his services to do that as well. And there goes Paul, scurrying about with a spraying machine, going from house to house, just as he said he would.

The Mammone family has returned to no power and a carpet of mud in the lower floor of the house. Nadine's mother is wielding a broom, shooing the mud outside. Nadine's 12-year-old son, Jack, declares he's never seen anything like it. Nadine shrugs and says, 'It's not as bad as I was

Above: A committed volunteer stands ankle-deep in stinking sludge on Saturday 15 January.

Left: A pontoon ripped from its moorings surges past Drift restaurant, which will eventually share the same fate.

anticipating.' But while they clean up their home, the Mammones will continue to stay at their friend's house.

At the Hayes household, Vilma is carrying out all the junk lying around their yard. Their house has escaped unscathed, with just the garage needing a clean-out. 'It's all washable,' Vilma says breezily. For now she has to clean up on her own; Paul is up the street, helping out another family.

Such is Paul's pace, I literally run after him to ask when he's heading home to help Vilma with their clean-up.

'Other people need a bit more help,' he replies. 'Ours is nothing, compared to some of the others. And my wife is quite capable.' He smiles and looks across at Vilma. 'Aren't you, dear?'

By way of contrition, he mutters, 'I'll open a nice bottle of red tonight.'

The Hayes are keenly aware they have something to toast with that red. For one, they have each other. They have lost very little, while others have lost so much. And, they believe, they have gained something from this flood – a greater appreciation of what it means to live in Gillan Street, Norman Park.

'We've made some wonderful friends out of it,' Paul and Vilma say of the flood. 'We've got to know everybody in the street. And we're looking forward to a big street party when it's all over.'

Over the next week or so I phone each of the residents I got to know, to see how they are faring.

Ten days after being flooded out, Nadine Mammone and her family have moved back in to a home that has no phone and limited power; downstairs is a skeleton of what it was. The walls have to be replaced. 'So we'll be living with plaster dust instead of mud,' Nadine says. And they're waiting for the insurance assessor to visit.

But the kids wanted to return home before starting school again.

'It will be like camping,' Nadine says. 'And the lovely Vilma has lent us a camp stove, so we can cook.'

Across the road, Ingrid Bailey is moving into a unit upstairs. She estimates she has lost about half her belongings, but 'it's just stuff. I'm going through a Zen minimalist stage!'

Instead, Ingrid is rejoicing at what the flood has brought her. Old friends, who heard about her plight via social networking, have got in touch with her, and she is embracing what she calls her 'sense of place'. In Gillan Street, Ingrid says, she has not only found a home but an understanding of what that means.

'I thought our street was close before the flood, but now it's even closer,' she explains.

'And I've found out one guy in the street has $350 bottles of wine! He thought he'd lost them during the flood, but his friend hid them as a practical joke during the clean-up. He did find them again!'

Above: Residents sandbag their waterfront home as the Brisbane River's water levels steadily climb on 11 January.

As for Paul and Vilma Hayes, they have turned adversity into an opportunity. The flood has pushed forward their plans to landscape the garden. During the clean-up, they met a young man called Nick, who has trained as an archaeologist and was helping out his friends further up the street. Paul and Vilma have employed Nick for a couple of weeks, to help them dig trenches.

'So he's no longer an archaeologist but a landscape gardener,' Vilma says.

Paul and Vilma say the fences have been cleaned, 'so we can't point and say this is where the water came to', and grass is sprouting once more along the verges. So the physical reminders of the flood are few.

'But we're still astounded by the volunteers,' Vilma says. 'All those people who helped clean up the yard, strangers turning up with food or offering to take away washing.'

For Kevin Rudd, his flood experience provided at least one painful legacy, an infected foot, which has healed.

Two and half weeks after he had waded into the heart of his electorate, the Foreign Minister shares a few of his thoughts on the phone from Switzerland. He says he has driven along Gillan Street since the flood and observed that it's 'approaching normality'. He and his office have been tying up the 'remaining loose ends', such as returning the bags to the Korean students.

Mr Rudd's efforts in Gillan Street have earned him an invitation to the street party. He plans to attend, and he expects Walter will tell him, 'I was right!'

And from the flood, Kevin Rudd holds hope that many have learnt that in confronting a common challenge, communities don't need to look far: they can turn to each other.

From Gillan Street to streets right across Brisbane and Queensland, he says, people have discovered what being a neighbour is about.

Certainly for the residents of this little cul-de-sac in Norman Park, and for many of those who helped them, that is the peak of the 2011 flood, when the spirit of a neighbourhood and a community rose higher than the water. And, unlike the mud on the fences, that spirit has left an indelible mark on the soul of Gillan Street.

last
words

Above: Floodwaters take over the ground floor level of high-set homes in Depot Hill, Rockhampton.

Previous page: Trevor Brownlie, a farmer from Theodore, inspects the remains of his ravaged cotton crop.

On 4 January, rising waters lap at the top step of a home in Depot Hill, Rockhampton.

ACKNOWLEDGEMENTS

It has been a great privilege for ABC Books/HarperCollins Publishers Australia to publish this book, both as a record of the floods and as a tribute to those affected by them. It would not have been possible without the enthusiasm, support and generosity of many people. We would like to acknowledge the invaluable contributions made by the following:

Premier Anna Bligh

The writers – Scott Bevan, Jenny Brennen, Richard Fidler, Peter Gunders, Spencer Howson, Jo Joyce, Madonna King, Paul Lockyer, Simon Marnie, Lisa Millar, Rhianna Patrick, Alice Roberts, Emma Sykes and Craig Zonca

The photographers – Sam Burgess, Arlie Douglas, Celine Foenander, Peter Giafis, Peter Gunders, Spencer Howson, Rhianna Patrick, Sally Rope, Alice Roberts, Sascha Rundle, Guilio Saggin, Belinda Sanders, Kaitlyn Sawrey, Emma Sykes, Jodie van de Wetering, Craig Zonca

Tony Rasmussen, Manager, Regional Local Radio; David Hua, Manager, Multiplatform Content, ABC Radio; and Scott Gamble, Editor, Multiplatform Content QLD, ABC Radio

Lynley Marshall, Director, ABC Commercial; Liz White, General Manager, ABC Publishing (Acting); Ellen Herlihy, Head, Strategy and Policy; and John Woodward, General Manager, Marketing and Communications

Richard Potter, who provided expert legal advice and kindly waived his fee

Graphic Print Group, for the generous donation of reproduction fees

The team from Red Hill Publishing – Sally Collings, Robert Collings, Gayna Murphy and Catherine Vallance

Opposite: The torrent tore away the brick facade of this Toowoomba apartment while one of the residents was at home. He managed to climb out a window into a neighbouring unit.

By 3 January, the swollen Fitzroy River has claimed East Street, Rockhampton.